Stable *to* Table

Happy trails to Ella!
Love, Dawn

Stable to Table

Menu Cookbook

RECIPES FROM AROUND THE EQUESTRIAN WORLD

Recipes and Food Styling
DAWN HARRIS BROWN

Project Editing and Text Design
CHRISTY SANANTONIO

Photography, Layout and Design
RACHEL CHOTIN LINCOLN

BROWNCROFT PUBLISHERS, L.L.C.

All rights reserved.
Published in the United States by Browncroft Publishers,
Browncroft L.L.C.

www.stabletotablecookbook.com

Many recipes in the book originally appeared in issues
of Southern Bridle Magazine

Library of Congress Cataloging-in Publication Data
is available by request.

ISBN 978-0-615-55140-1

Printed in China

Design by Rachel Chotin Lincoln
Photograph credits appear on page 130.

First Edition January 2012

Table of Contents

The United States of America

AMERICAN RACING THOROUGHBRED HORSE

Kentucky Mint Julep
Hall of Fame Mint Tea
Winner's Spicy Pecans
Tallyho Cocktail
Triple Crown Hors d'oeuvres
Bluegrass Filet of Beef & Romaine Salad
Kentucky Hot Mrs. Brown & Broiled Herb-Stuffed Tomato
Derby Pie
Demitasse

AMERICAN PAINT HORSE
POLO PONY
AMERICAN QUARTER HORSE
APPALOOSA

Lady Bird's Texas Beef Chili
Chipotle Guacamole
Lidaritas
Cilantro Pesto
Coriander Chicken Tostados with Refried Beans
Sugared Flour Tortillas
Sliced Oranges with Honey and Cinnamon

Stable *to* Table

Stable *to* Table

Kentucky Mint Julep

Kentucky Bourbon
crushed ice
chilled silver tumbler
3 or 4 3 inch long sprigs of mint
1 ½ tsp simple syrup (brew to consistency of honey)

1. In a prechilled polished silver tumbler, rub a sprig of mint with firm, though gentle, pressure around the inside of the tumbler, being careful not to crush the leaves.
2. Brew equal parts of sugar and water to a consistency of honey. Pour a teaspoon and a half slowly over the ice.
3. Fill the tumbler with the finest Bourbon.
4. Stir until frost appears. Top with sprigs of mint and serve.

Hall of Fame Mint Tea

2 cups sugar
2 ½ cups water
1 cup firmly packed mint leaves
juice of 6 lemons
juice of 2 oranges
rind of 1 orange, grated

1. Boil sugar and water 5 minutes. Cool; add remaining ingredients and let stand for 1 hour.
2. Strain and refrigerate.
3. To serve, combine one part juice mixture with 2 parts brewed tea.
4. Pour over crushed ice in glasses. Serves 36.
   Omit orange juice and rind for lemonade tea.

Winner's Spicy Pecans

4 tbsp butter
½ tsp cayenne pepper
2 tsp Cajun seasoning
2 tsp ground cumin
5 tbsp sugar
1 lb. pecans

1. Melt butter in skillet over medium-high.
2. Add cayenne, cajun seasoning, cumin, and sugar. Mix well, then add the pecans.
3. Cook about 3 minutes stirring until lightly colored.
4. Pour the pecans onto wire rack, placed over baking sheet.
5. Cool to room temperature. Store in airtight container until ready to serve. Warm before serving.

Tallyho Cocktail

2 oz. Grenadine	2 oz. Rum
2 oz. Sloe gin	juice of 1 lime
2 oz. Triple Sec	2 cups of crushed ice

1. Blend all ingredients for 30 seconds.
2. Pour into a martini glass.
3. Decorate with a continuous peeled lime to attach to lip of glass and entwined around the stem. Attach a cherry on the top of the lime. Serve immediately.

Thoroughbred

Stable *to* Table

Savory Pimento Cheese Sandwiches

2 lbs. sharp cheddar cheese, coarsely shredded
2 jars pimientos (8 oz. total) drained, diced
1 ½ cups mayonnaise, or less
1 small white onion finely chopped
1 tsp lemon juice
1 tsp coarsely ground black pepper

1. Thoroughly combine all ingredients, using just enough mayonnaise to achieve desired consistency.
2. Spread on white bread rounds or triangles for a true Southern delight.

Sweet Onion Sandwiches

firm white bread, thinly sliced
mayonnaise
sweet mild onions (Vidalia), thinly sliced
freshly ground black pepper to taste
minced fresh parsley

1. Cut bread into circles - do not use the crust.
2. Thinly coat one side of each circle with mayonnaise.
3. For each sandwich, place one onion slice on a bread circle, sprinkle with salt and pepper, and top with another circle.
4. Brush the edge of each sandwich with mayonnaise, then roll the edge in minced parsley.
5. Arrange sandwiches on a platter and cover with a damp dish towel until ready to serve.

Kentucky Country Ham on Tiny Biscuits

2 cups all-purpose flour
1 tbsp Baking powder
1 tsp salt
½ cup vegetable shortening
1 cup milk

1. Sift together flour, baking powder, and salt in a large bowl. Cut in shortening until mixture resembles course crumbs. Add just enough milk to moisten all ingredients.
2. Place on a floured surface. Knead, if necessary, to get dough to hold together. Roll out to ¼ inch thickness.
3. Cut with a 2 inch or less biscuit cutter and place on an ungreased baking sheet. Bake at 450° F for 20 minutes or until lightly browned. Yields 1 ½ dozen biscuits.
4. Thinly slice the baked ham and sandwich between hot tiny biscuits.
   To freeze, bake only 15 minutes, not allowing biscuits to brown. Wrap cooled biscuits tightly in plastic. To serve, thaw completely and bake at 450° F for 10-15 minutes until lightly brown.

Romaine Salad with Horseradish-Blue Cheese Dressing

¼ cup sour cream

½ cup mayonnaise

1 teaspoon prepared horseradish

1 tablespoon lemon juice

2/3 cup blue cheese crumbled

8 cups romaine lettuce, cut into bite size pieces

1 teaspoon lemon zest

2/3 pint cherry tomatoes, sliced lengthwise

½ cup red onion, thinly sliced

1. In a small bowl, mix together the sour cream, mayonnaise, horseradish, lemon juice, and ½ teaspoon pepper using a hand held wire whisk. Season the dressing with salt and pepper, if necessary, and reserve.
2. In a large bowl, toss together the lettuce, lemon zest, tomatoes, half the cheese, and the dressing.
3. Divide the mixture among 8 individual plates.

Bluegrass Filet of Beef

3 lbs. of filet of beef tenderloin

Cracked pepper

Salt

½ stick of soften butter

1. Trim all the fat from the tenderloin. Pat dry. Tie the beef with cotton string at 1 inch apart.
2. Press the cracked pepper and salt into the meat.
3. Rub the entire meat with soften butter.
4. Roast meat at 400° F for 5 min., reduce oven to 350° F to desired degree of doneness, 45 min. for medium rare (meat thermometer should read 140-145° F).
5. Allow beef to rest for 20 minutes before cutting. Slice beef diagonally in ¼" slices.
6. Place the sliced steak around the salad and top with the onion slices and remaining cheese. Serves 8 with hearty flavors that are both easy to prepare and beautiful to present.

Kentucky Hot Mrs. Brown

    4 slices whole grained bread toasted
    4 slices of roasted chicken breast or turkey breast
    sliced
    8 slices of thick bacon
    ¾ cup grated Gruyere cheese
    1 bunch of trimmed and poached asparagus drained

1. Place toast on a lined cookie sheet, cover with drained
   cooked tender asparagus, add sliced chicken or turkey.
   Top with cheese sauce and sprinkle on more cheese.
   Place almost cooked bacon crisscrossed on top. Place
   under broiler and broil slowly until bacon is crisp.
2. Plate the "Hot Mrs. Brown" with a Broiled Herb-Stuffed
   tomato. Toast points on the side. Serves 4.
   *This is Mrs. Dawn Brown's twist on the famous Kentucky
   Hot Brown originating from the Brown Hotel.*

CHEESE SAUCE

2 tbsp whole milk
2 tbsp flour
½ cup Gruyere grated cheese
1 tsp Sriracha hot chili sauce
¼ tsp salt
*Melt butter in saucepan, blend in flour. Add milk, cheese,
and seasonings, stirring constantly until smooth and thick.
Set aside.*

Broiled Herb-Stuffed Tomato

    4 stemmed medium tomatoes
    1 shallot finely chopped
    1 clove of garlic finely chopped
    2 tbsp fresh basil shredded
    1 tbsp fresh parsley
    2 tbsp olive oil
    1 cup of panko (Japanese breadcrumbs)
    3 tbsp real crumbled bacon

1. Remove the tops from the tomatoes and core. Retain
   the tops with the stems.
2. In a small bowl, mix all ingredients.
3. Divide the herb mixture among the tomatoes, then
   place in a baking pan.
4. Drizzle with a few drops of the olive oil and broil at
   450° F for 6 minutes or until browned. Serve with the
   Kentucky Hot Mrs. Brown

Derby Pie & Demitasse

1 cup light brown sugar
1 cup dark corn syrup
½ stick butter melted
4 eggs beaten
¼ cup Bourbon
Pinch of salt
1 unbaked 9-inch pie crust
1 to 1 ¼ cups pecan halves
½ cup mini chocolate morsels

1. Combine first 3 ingredients to the beaten eggs.
2. Whisk in the Bourbon and salt to the mixture.
3. Sprinkle the mini morsels evenly over pie shell.
4. Top with the pecans then pour liquid mixture carefully over pecans.
5. Bake at 400° F for 15 min. then lower oven to 350° F for 30 min. or until firm.

If you dare fiddle with such a monument to Southern culinary culture then try a dollop of bourbon flavored whipped cream on the side.

Stable *to* Table

Thoroughbred

Stable *to* Table

Lady Bird's Texas Beef Chili

4 lb. chili meat
(coarsely ground round steak or well-trimmed chuck)
1 large onion, chopped
2 cloves of garlic
1 tsp oregano
1 tsp cumin
6 tsp chili powder (or more)
2 cans (20oz. each) tomatoes
2 to 6 generous dashes hot pepper sauce
salt
2 cups hot water

1. Place meat, onion, and garlic with 2 tablespoons of bacon fat in a large heavy skillet or Dutch oven. Cook until meat is light-colored.
2. Add remaining ingredients. Bring to a boil, lower heat and simmer, uncovered about an hour. Skim fat during cooking.
3. If you like it thicker stir in ¼ c finely ground cornmeal.
4. Cover top with tortilla chips and cheese. Run under broiler to melt cheese.
5. Serve Texas-style with guacamole, jalapenos, cilantro and pico de gallo. Serves 10 to 12.
Mrs. Johnson gave this recipe to my mother, Mrs. Harris, in the 1960's. I can't find a better chili recipe than this …remember it's always better the next day when all the spices blend!

Chipotle Guacamole

2 tbsp finely minced white onion
1 tbsp fresh lime juice
1 tomato seeded, chopped
1 to 2 chipotle chilies in abodo, drained and minced
½ tsp sea salt
2 large Haas avocados
2 tbsp finely minced cilantro
1 tbsp fresh cilantro leaves

1. Put the minced onion, lime juice, chipotle chilies, tomatoes and the ½ tsp. salt in a molcajete or small bowl, and smash with a pestle or fork to a course paste.
2. Cut the avocados in half, remove the pits and scoop out the flesh into the molcajete.
3. Add the minced cilantro and mix leaving some lumps. Taste and adjust seasonings with salt.
4. Sprinkle the guacamole with cilantro leaves and serve immediately, if possible. Makes about 2 cups.
To keep the guacamole at room temperature for up to an hour, cover with plastic wrap, pressing it directly onto the surface. To keep the guacamole for up to 3 hours, do not add the cilantro until just before serving and cover and store in the refrigerator.

Cilantro Pesto

1 tbsp chopped garlic
¼ cup freshly grated parmesan cheese
1 cup cilantro leaves
3 tbsp pepitas (pumpkin seeds)
2 tbsp olive oil
¼ tsp salt
juice of ½ lime

1. Grind all ingredients together in a blender or food processor to form a paste.
2. Use on scrambled eggs, pasta, or a dip with tortilla chips.

Lidaritas

2 oz. fresh lime juice (best with key limes)
4 oz. Hiram Walker Triple Sec (48 or 60 proof)
4 oz. 100% Agave Tequila or Sauza Hornitos

1. Rim glasses with salt.
2. Stir and pour over crushed ice.

Famous Margarita recipe from Lida McAllister

Cutting Horse

Stable to Table

American Paint

The United States of America

Stable *to* Table

Skull Valley Polo Club, Arizona

Dr. C. Paul Harris, Sr., 1938

The United States of America

23

American Quarter

American Quarter

Coriander Chicken Tostados with Refried Beans

BEANS:

2 (15 oz.) cans of pinto beans
(liquid drained and reserved)

½ cup chopped white onion

2 tbsp dried oregano

2 garlic cloves, peeled

2 tsp minced canned chipotle chiles in Adobo

1 tbsp extra virgin olive oil

course Kosher salt

CHICKEN:

4 skinless chicken breast halves

½ cup coriander seeds coarsely crushed in plastic bag

ASSEMBLY:

6 purchased corn tostada shells

3 cups thinly sliced romaine lettuce

6 radishes, sliced thin

6 fresh cilantro sprigs

lime wedges

1. Place beans, onion, oregano, garlic, chipotle chiles and olive oil in processor; blend to chunky puree.
2. Heat oil in heavy saucepan over medium heat. Add bean mixture and ½ cup of bean liquid.
3. Stir over medium heat until warmed through, adding more bean liquid if dry. Season with salt and pepper.
4. Flatten chicken with rolling pin between plastic wrap.
5. Crush coriander seeds.
6. Sprinkle chicken with salt, pepper and coriander seeds.
7. Saute chicken in the oil about 3 minutes per side. Cool 5 minutes and slice lengthwise in 1/3 in. strips.
8. Top each tostada shell with beans, lettuce, radishes, chicken, and cilantro sprig. Serve with lime wedges.

The United States of America

Sugared Flour Tortillas

    flour tortillas

    oil for frying

    cinnamon and sugar

1. Fry tortillas in hot oil until golden.
2. Drain on paper towels and sprinkle with a mixture of sugar and cinnamon.

Sliced Oranges with Honey and Cinnamon

    6 navel oranges peeled and sliced in rings

    ½ cup honey

    1 tsp cinnamon

    mint sprigs for garnish

1. Slice oranges on a round plate.
2. Stir cinnamon in honey and drizzle over oranges.
3. Garnish with mint.

27

Austria

LIPIZZAN HORSE   Wiener Schnitzel
Erdapfelsalat (Austrian Potato Salad)
Sachertorte (Viennese Chocolate Cake)

Wiener Schnitzel

2 pounds veal
(cut into steaks)
salt and pepper
1 cup flour
3 eggs
2 cups bread crumbs
¼ cup oil for frying

1. Salt and pepper the veal steaks and pound the meat very thin (¼ inch).
2. Roll steaks in flour shaking excess off. Dip floured veal into the beaten eggs and then into the bread crumbs.
3. Bring oil to frying temperature and brown steaks for 2 minutes each side. Drain on paper towels. Change oil with each batch of steaks so there are no burned bread crumbs. Serve with potato salad and red cabbage slaw. Serves 8.

Erdapfelsalat (Austrian Potato Salad)

1 pound small potatoes (golden, red or fingerling)
1 cup finely chopped onion
1 tsp Dijon mustard
2 tbsp vinegar
½ cup chopped parsley
5 tbsp oil
salt and pepper

1. Boil potatoes until tender. Drain and cut in half.
2. Add the finely chopped onion to the potatoes.
3. Whisk the mustard with the vinegar, then slowly add the oil. Pour over the still warm potatoes.
4. Sprinkle with the parsley, salt and pepper to taste.
5. Serve at room temperature. Serves 8.

Lippizan

Austria

Lippizan

Stable *to* Table

Sachertorte (Viennese Chocolate Cake)

1 devil's food cake mix
1 cup apricot preserves
1 tbsp apricot liquor or rum
6 oz. bittersweet chocolate
2 tbsp butter
¼ cup heavy cream (preheated)

1. Prepare cake mix as directed on box.
2. Pour into an 9" round cake pan lined and buttered on the bottom of pan. Bake until a toothpick comes out clean. Let rest for 5 mins., then invert on a parchment lined board.
3. Remove the lining paper and let cool. Cake will shrink and the top will flatten.
4. Turn cake over and cut the top, if needed, to a flat surface.
5. When cake is completely cool, cut in half using short strokes all around the cake.

6. Bring the apricot preserves and rum to a boil in a small sauce pan.
7. Brush the cake half with the mixture, put the top layer on evenly and brush the top and sides. Let set.
Place short pieces of parchment paper under the perimeter of cake before icing for easy cleanup.

CHOCOLATE GLAZE

Place a metal mixing bowl over a pan of simmering water. Chop chocolate into small pieces and melt in bowl with the butter. When melted, whisk in the preheated hot cream. Remove bowl from the simmering water and let glaze cool to a spreading consistency. Pour glaze over cake and spread with an icing knife evenly on top and sides. Remove the short pieces of parchment paper.
Sachertortes traditionally have no decoration.

Austria

Colombia

PASO FINO HORSE   Ajiaco (Chicken, Corn, and Potato Soup)
Arepas (Corn Meal Cakes)
Dulce de Leche (Fig, Cheese, and Caramel Cream)

Ajiaco (Chicken, Corn and Potato Soup)

2 whole chicken breasts

4 cups chicken broth

I onion chopped

salt

pepper

2 lbs. peeled and diced potatoes

2 tbsp of the herb guascas or cilantro

I clove of garlic minced

3 ears of corn cut in 3 inch lengths

I ear of corn kernels cut off the cob

GARNISH
capers, crema de leche (clotted cream)
slice of avocado

1. Cook the chicken, covered, until tender in the broth with the chopped onion, salt and pepper. When the chicken is done, remove from broth and shred. Set aside in a bowl.
2. Cook the peeled and diced potatoes, guascas or cilantro, minced garlic, and corn in remaining chicken broth. Simmer for 45 minutes or until the vegetables are tender.
3. Serve the hot soup topped with the shredded chicken along with small bowls of capers, heavy cream, a slice of avocado and arepas. Serves 6.

Arepas (Corn Cakes)

I cup pre-cooked white corn mix (found in most supermarkets under arepas mix)

pinch of sugar

pinch of salt

I cup shredded mozzarella cheese

I cup milk

3 tbsp melted butter

1. Mix corn mix with the sugar, salt and cheese in a mixing bowl.
2. Add the warmed milk and butter. Mix until the ingredients are incorporated. Knead for about 5 minutes until smooth.
3. Roll into golf-ball size pieces. Place (one at a time) into a plastic sandwich bag and flatten with a cutting board.
4. While still in the bag, cut with a drinking glass to form the round cake.
5. When all the dough rounds have been cut, cook on a non-stick grill or skillet until lightly browned on each side. Serve immediately while still hot.
A Colombian meal is not complete without arepas!

Colombia

Dulce de Leche
(Fig, Cheese, and Caramel Cream)

fresh black figs or fig preserves

Manchego cheese (or any white cheese)

1 tbsp dulce de leche

1. Cut figs and cheese to desired size.
2. Arrange all ingredients on a serving dish.

   A very typical finish for a Colombian meal are black figs from the Colombian mountains, Manchego cheese and dulce de leche. Dulce de leche can be found in the chocolate syrup section of the grocery.

Paso Fino

39

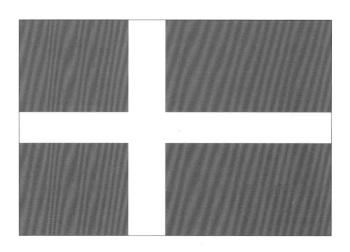

Denmark

DANISH WARMBLOOD HORSE

The Danish Open-Faced Sandwich
Frikadeller (Danish Meatballs)
Rod Kal (Braised Red Cabbage)
Fiskefrikadeller (Fish Cakes)
Agurkesalat (Cucumber Salad)
Kartoffelsalat (Potato Salad)
Ris a l-amande med arm kirsebaer sovs
(Rice and Almond Pudding with Cherry Sauce)

The Danish Open-Faced Sandwich

The traditional Danish open sandwich or *smorrebrod* always starts with bread and sweet Danish butter. The legend of the sandwich, some say, started with the medieval custom of eating off bread instead of plates… the leftovers given to the village poor to eat. Today, the sandwiches are the Danish fast food for their lunch breaks. There are many restaurants offering exclusively open sandwiches in classic combinations. Bread is sour rye, dark, moist, tight in texture, only 1/8 inch thick and buttered evenly and thickly, since the butter acts as a juice-proof seal. Combinations of bibb lettuce, meat, fish, cheese, baby shrimp, pate, eggs and garnishes for flavor and texture. When making sandwiches for guests, be sure to make at least three kinds. Serve on a wooden board or decorative platter. Start with fish sandwiches first, then move on to meat options.

1. Pickled herring with onion rings, lettuce and a sliver of tomato, on rye bread.
2. Sliced roast pork garnished with pork crackling, prunes and a curl of orange, on rye bread.
3. Sliced hard-boiled eggs and tomatoes sprinkled with chives, on lettuce-covered rye bread.
4. Small Danish shrimp on a bed of lettuce, topped with a slice of lemon, on white bread.
5. Liver pate and sautéed mushroom slices, a strip of bacon and a lettuce leaf, on rye bread.
6. Sliced meatballs (frikadeller) topped with pickled beets and a cucumber slice, on rye bread.
7. Smoked salmon and scrambled eggs sprinkled with chives, on white bread.
8. Roast beef and pickles on a bed of lettuce, on rye bread.
9. Salami rounds and onion rings with a sprig of parsley, on rye bread.
10. Danish blue cheese with a slice of hard-boiled egg encircled by an onion ring, on white bread.

Danish Warmblood

Frikadeller (Danish Meatballs)

2 eggs
8 oz. ground veal
8 oz. ground pork
½ cup fine breadcrumbs
½ cup finely chopped onion
1 cup milk
6 tbsp butter
salt and ground pepper

1. Beat eggs in a small bowl. In a larger bowl mix meats, breadcrumbs and chopped onion until blended. Mix in eggs (it might be easier to mix with your hands).
2. Add milk, salt and pepper in the bowl and continue to mix. Refrigerate mixture for 30 min.
3. Make the balls. Form 16-20 oval patties.
4. Melt butter in large frying pan. Cook meatballs for 8-10 minutes, in batches of 4 or 5 until golden brown. Pork should be cooked thoroughly and not pink in the middle. Keep warm until meatballs are cooked. Serve immediately. These can be frozen and reheated in the oven.

Many Danes consider frikadeller to be the national dish. Every cook makes the basic recipe with their own twist. It's traditionally served with gravy, rye bread, dill pickles, boiled potatoes, and red cabbage or pickled beets.

Rod Kal (Braised Red Cabbage)

3 lbs. red cabbage
¼ cup distilled white vinegar
2 tbsp butter
1 medium onion, chopped
2 tart apples cored and thinly sliced
¼ cup sugar
½ cup currant juice or apple juice
¼ tsp ground allspice
6 whole cloves
salt

1. Shred cabbage and place in a large pan. Add ½ cup of vinegar and bring to a boil. Reduce heat and simmer for 1 hour. Careful not to scorch.
2. Meanwhile, melt the butter in a large frying pan over medium heat. Stir in onion and apple and cook for 5-7 minutes until soft.
3. Stir in the apples and onions into the cabbage with sugar, juice, allspice and cloves. Add salt. Simmer gently for 1 1/2 hours. Serves 6.

This dish is very popular all over Scandinavia. Vibrant red cabbage compliments any dish in taste as well as a visual.

Agurkesalat (Cucumber Salad)

1 large English cucumber (14 inches)
5 tbsp distilled white vinegar
2 tbsp white sugar
3 tbsp chopped fresh dill
salt and ground white pepper to taste

1. Slice cucumber into 1/8 in. pieces in a serving bowl.
2. Combine the vinegar, sugar and dill in a small bowl and season with salt and pepper. Pour over cucumbers and toss. Chill.

Denmark has always included cucumbers as a favorite food. Make the salad right when about to serve to retain its crispness. One cup of sour cream can also be added for a richer dressing. Always good with all fish dishes.

Fiskefrikadeller (Fish Cakes)

1 lb. cod
8 oz. salmon fillet
6 oz. smoked salmon
2 tbsp finely chopped onion
3 tbsp melted butter
3 eggs
¼ cup all-purpose flour
salt and white pepper

1. Place fish in shallow dish, sprinkled with salt to draw out moisture. Pat dry.
2. Put all fish in a food processor. Add onion, butter, eggs and flour. Pulse until smooth, season with salt and pepper.
3. Preheat oven to 375° F. Lightly grease baking tray. Form fish mixture into patties and place on tray.
4. Bake fish cakes for 30-35 minutes, until they are cooked through and lightly browned. Serve immediately. Serves 4.

Fish cakes are another Danish favorite. Serve with remoulade, buttered potatoes and pickled cucumber salad.

Danish Warmblood

Kartoffelsalat (Potato Salad)

4 lb. potatoes
3 tbsp finely chopped onion
2 celery stalks, finely chopped
I cup sour cream
I cup mayonnaise
I tsp dried mustard
I tsp celery seed
5 tbsp chopped fresh dill
salt and pepper

1. I. Boil the potatoes in lightly salted water for 20 min. or until tender. Drain and cool. Peel and coarsely chop in a large bowl. Add onion and celery.

2. Make dressing in separate bowl. Mix sour cream, mayonnaise, mustard, celery seed, dill, salt and pepper.

3. Add dressing to the potatoes, toss gently, cover bowl and chill until ready to serve. Serves 6-8.

The potato is a Danish staple as well as other Scandinavian countries.

Denmark

Ris a lamented med varm kirsebaer sovs (Rice and Almond Pudding with Cherry Sauce)

1 quart whole milk
4 tbsp sugar
¾ cup white rice
1/3 cup blanched and chopped almonds
2 tsp vanilla
1 cup heavy cream
1 whole almond

1. Bring the milk to a boil in a 2-quart saucepan and add the sugar and rice. Stir once or twice, then lower the heat and simmer uncovered about 25 minutes, or until the rice is quite soft and not mushy. *(Cooking time for rice varies, but a sure test is to rub a grain between the thumb and first finger; if there is not a hard kernel in the center, the rice is done.)*
2. Pour the rice immediately into a bowl to cool it quickly, and then add the chopped almonds and vanilla.
3. Whip the heavy cream in a chilled bowl until it thickens and holds soft peaks.
4. Fold whipped cream into tepid rice mixture, turn the pudding into a serving dish and chill before serving.

CHERRY SAUCE

1 lb. fresh or bottled dark cherries
(stoned and cut into quarters)
2 cups of water
½ cup sugar
1 tsp fresh lemon juice
2 whole cloves
2 tbsp cornstarch

Put cherries into a saucepan with the water, sugar, lemon juice, and cloves. Cook gently for 20 minutes. Put a small amount of the cherry juice into a small bowl. Add the cornstarch to the juice and blend into a paste. Stir the cornstarch mixture into the cherries and cook for 10 min., until thickened. Remove from the heat and cool. Drizzle over the rice pudding for a traditional Christmas dessert.

Serves 8. Be sure to put a lucky whole almond into the pudding so the fortunate person can claim his prize!

Danish Warmblood

Denmark

49

France

CAMARGUE HORSE
SELLE FRANCAIS HORSE

Vineyard Roasted Game Hens

Potatoes au Gratin

Roasted Eggplant, Tomato and Onion

White Asparagus with Egg, Lemon and Butter Sauce

Pear Tart

Vineyard Roasted Game Hens

2 oven ready game hens or pheasants
salt and pepper
sprigs of thyme
4 tbsp butter
½ cup dry white wine
1 small red onion or shallot, chopped
4 tbsp heavy cream or creme fraiche
½ cup seeded red grapes sliced

1. Season birds with salt and pepper and place thyme inside each.
2. Melt half the butter in a cast iron casserole and brown birds lightly all over.
3. Add wine, cover and cook over low heat or in a 350° F oven for 40 to 50 minutes or until cooked to your preference. Transfer birds to a serving dish.
4. Melt the remaining butter in the pan and cook the onion until soft. Add the grapes and cook for 3 minutes.
5. Remove sauce from heat and stir in cream.
6. Spoon sauce over birds and garnish with remaining thyme. Serves 4 to 6.

Stable *to* Table

France

53

Camargue

Stable *to* Table

Potatoes au Gratin

5 medium potatoes
nutmeg
salt and pepper
1 clove of garlic
1 cup half and half cream
2 tbsp butter, cut in small pieces
2 cups Gruyere or Swiss cheese

1. Preheat oven to 400° F.
2. Peel potatoes, wash, and wipe dry. Slice the into ¼" slices.
3. In a large saucepan add potatoes and cover with water. Bring water and potatoes to a boil, then lower heat to a simmer for 20 to 25 minutes or until the potatoes are tender.
4. Drain the potatoes when done and place ½ of them in a baking dish rubbed with the clove of garlic.
5. Add a layer of potatoes, sprinkle with cheese, salt, pepper, and nutmeg and half the cream. Then, another layer of potatoes, spices, and finishing with cheese.
6. Dot the butter on top.
7. Carefully pour the remainder of the cream around the sides.
8. Place the dish in the oven and bake for 45 minutes, or until the surface is golden brown.

Roasted Eggplant, Tomato and Onion

2 small eggplants about 1 lb. sliced

1 red onion sliced

1 lb. tomatoes about 3

1 clove garlic

1 tsp thyme leaves

1 small bay leaf crushed

¼ cup olive oil

salt and pepper

1. Preheat the oven to 425° F.
2. Wash and dry vegetables, then slice them about ½" thick.
3. Place in an oiled baking dish alternating onion, tomato and eggplant decoratively making parallel lines of vegetables overlapping. Sprinkle a little of the garlic, thyme, bay leaf, salt and pepper between slices.
4. Drizzle the olive oil over all and bake for 20 to 30 minutes or until lightly golden on top. If they are too dry, cover with foil during the last 10 minutes of cooking time. *A final sprinkling of parmesan cheese is a nice finish.*

Selle Francais

France

Asparagus with Egg and Lemon, Butter Sauce

2 lbs. white or green asparagus stems peeled and trimmed

3 eggs

½ cup butter

juice of 1 lemon

salt and pepper

1. Peel and trim the asparagus. Simmer in salted boiling water for 6 to 10 minutes. *Depending on size, a sharp knife should go into the stalk easily.*

2. Drain the asparagus and place on a serving dish.

3. Hard boil 2 eggs. Reserve to grate or chop on top.

4. Put a metal bowl over a pot of simmering water. Beat an egg yolk with the lemon juice then slowly add the melted butter beating constantly. *Never let the boiling water touch the bowl.*

5. Remove from steam and beat to a sauce consistency. Pour over asparagus and garnish with the grated or chopped hard boiled egg. Serves 6 to 8.

Pear Tart

    1 prepared pie shell
    1 ¾ half and half cream
    ½ cup of sugar
    2 eggs and 1 egg yolk
    1 tsp vanilla
    3 pears

1. Arrange pie shell in an 8" tart pan
2. Peel and half the pears. Cut lengthwise, and slice horizontally.
3. Place on unbaked dough with the narrow part of the pear slices facing the middle. Gently press on slices for a fan shape.
4. Beat other ingredients with a whisk and pour over arranged pears.
5. Bake at 350° F for about 35 min. until set. *Recipe can be made with any combination of fruit and nuts.*

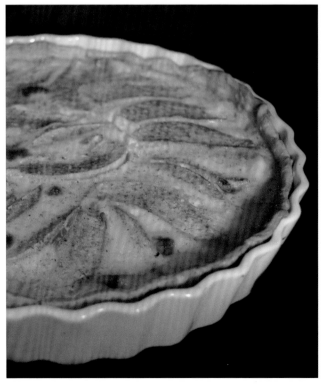

France

Germany

HANOVERIAN
TRAKEHNER
OLDENBERG

Konigssberger Klopse (Meatballs with Cream Sauce)
Winter Greens Salad with German "French" Dressing
German Sausage and Ham Plate
Kris' Apple Cake

Hanoverian

Stable *to* Table

Konigssberger Klopse
(Meatballs with Cream Sauce)

1 cup coarse fresh breadcrumbs
(made from staled sourdough bread)
¼ cup warmed milk
2 lbs. ground pork or veal
1 cup finely chopped onion
1 egg beaten
2 slices of finely chopped bacon
2 quarts or 8 cups of vegetable stock
large pinch of ground allspice
2 bay leaves
4 tbsp butter
5 tbsp plain flour
4 tbsp capers, rinsed
3 tbsp coarsely chopped parsley, extra for garnish
1 tbsp wholegrain mustard
zest and juice of 1 lemon
½ cup cream
2 egg yolks

Can be accompanied by boiled Yukon gold potatoes (yellow potatoes) and a bitter green salad – a nice mustard vinaigrette goes well.

1. Place the breadcrumbs and milk in a large bowl and mix well so the breadcrumbs absorb the milk. Add the ground meat, eggs and bacon and half the chopped onion. Season well with the salt and freshly ground pepper. Mix well then, using wet hands, form into 24 golfball sized meatballs. Set aside.

2. Put the other half of the onion in a large wide saucepan, along with the stock, allspice and bay leaves. Bring to a boil. Add meatballs, bring to a boil again, then simmer for 20 minutes. Remove the meatballs with a slotted spoon. Keep warm.

3. Strain the stock and reserve 4 cups and pour into a clean saucepan. Bring to a boil.

4. Meanwhile in another saucepan, gently melt the butter over medium heat then stir in the flour. Cook, stirring for 2-3 minutes. Fragrant but not browned.

5. Slowly whisk in the hot stock, making sure there are no lumps. Bring to a boil, stirring for 5 minutes.

6. Stir in the capers, parsley, mustard, lemon zest and juice into the stock mixture.

7. Place the cream and egg yolks in a bowl and whisk to combine. Remove the sauce for the heat and whisk in the cream sauce.

8. Gently mix in the warm meatballs. Taste, then season, and sprinkle with parsley. Serve immediately.
Serves 6.

Stable *to* Table

Trakehner

Winter Greens Salad
with German "French" Dressing

I tsp salt

plenty of ground pepper

I tsp mustard

I ¼ cup of olive oil

1/3 cup vinegar

I tsp sugar

I egg or 2 tbsp cream

stock or water

fresh salad greens

1. Blend together all the ingredients except the stock and greens in a blender or food processor until smooth. This makes a creamy, fairly thick dressing.
2. Add enough stock or water to give a lighter consistency.
3. Keep refrigerated in a screw top jar and use within 3-4 days. Makes about 2 cups
4. Toss with fresh salad greens.

German Sausage and Ham Plate

2 smoked ham hocks
1 lb. bratwurst sausages
1 lb. smoked sausages
½ lb. smoked bacon
2 onions
6 potatoes
1 small head of cabbage cut into wedges
1 clove garlic
2 bay leaves
2 cloves
salt and pepper

1. Simmer the ham hocks and bacon along with the quartered onions, bay leaves, garlic and cloves in enough water to cover for 1 hour.
2. Peel the potatoes and boil until done (about 20 min.).
3. Poach the sausages with the ham hocks for 10 min. Add the cabbage for 15 minutes.
4. Arrange the sausages, potatoes and cabbage on a platter.
5. Serve with horseradish, gherkins, pickled onions, and a variety of mustards.
Serves 6.

Oldenberg

Germany

Stable *to* Table

© Sparagowski

Oldenberg

Kris' Apple Cake

2 cups sugar

3 eggs

1 ½ cups vegetable oil

3 cups plain flour

1 ½ tsp baking soda

½ tsp each cinnamon, nutmeg, clove and salt

1 tsp vanilla extract

3 cups chopped apple (you can leave the skin on)

1 cup nuts (optional) walnuts, pecans or macadamias are a good choice

1. Mix sugar, eggs, vanilla and then add oil until completely blended.
2. Sift dry ingredients. Mix in with egg mixture
3. Add apples and nuts – mix with a wooden spoon
4. Grease and flour a bundt pan – add batter.
5. Bake in 350° F oven for 1 ¼ hours.
   Ready when a skewer comes out clean
6. Decorate with a drizzle of simple white icing and top with extra nuts. *Or, sift icing sugar over the top.*

SIMPLE WHITE ICING

Mix ½ cup confectioner's sugar and a few tbsp milk until you reach the right consistency

Great Britain

HACKNEY PONY
SHETLAND PONY
WELSH COB

Scotch Eggs
Shepherd's Pie
Fish and Chips
British Tea (Scones and Cucumber Sandwiches)

Scotch Eggs

8 hard boiled eggs

1 lb. bulk sausage

flour

breadcrumbs

beaten egg

oil for frying

1. Heat oil to 375° F.
2. Roll eggs in flour and shake off excess.
3. Press the sausage around egg.
4. Dip in beaten egg and roll in breadcrumbs.
5. Fry in oil, turning often to brown the sausage.
6. Eat warm or room temp. Cut in half to serve. Serves 8.

Hackney Pony

Stable *to* Table

Shepherd's Pie

2 lbs. ground beef or lamb (lean)

1 cup onion chopped

½ cup diced bell pepper

½ cup chopped celery

2 grated carrots

2 tbsp Worchestershire sauce

½ cup red wine

½ cup beef broth

1 (6 oz.) can of tomato paste

salt and pepper

3 ½ lbs potatoes

4 tbsp butter

½ cup milk (warm)

½ cup parmesan cheese grated

2 tbsp butter to dot on top

2 eggs beaten

1. Brown meat in large heavy skillet. Add onion, bell pepper, celery, and carrots. Cook until vegetables are soft.
2. Add the worchestershire sauce, red wine and tomato paste and beef broth. Simmer until mixture is thick, about 15 minutes.
3. Peel and boil potatoes. Mash with the butter, milk, parmesan cheese and beaten eggs.
4. Put meat mixture in a casserole dish and cover with the mashed potatoes. Dot with the remainder butter.
5. Bake in a 425° F oven until the potatoes are golden brown. Serves 8.

Great Britain

Shetland Pony

Fish and Chips

2 cups sifted flour

1 ½ tsp salt

¼ tsp freshly ground black pepper

4 eggs, separated

1 can beer

½ cup butter, melted

bite-size cod or other firm fish

oil for deep frying

1. Sift together the flour, salt, and pepper. Set aside.
2. Beat egg yolks until light. Add the beer and mix into the dry ingredients, stirring only until blended.
3. Stir in butter and let stand at room temperature 1 ½ hours.
4. Beat egg whites until stiff and fold into batter.
5. Heat oil to 375° F.
6. Dip fish into batter and fry until golden brown, about 2 to 3 minutes. Serves 6 to 8.

CHIPS

2 lbs. potatoes

salt and pepper

1 tbsp of oil

1. Preheat oven to 450° F.
2. Peel and dry potatoes. Slice potatoes lengthwise into wedges. Toss with oil, salt and pepper.
3. Heat sheet pan in the oven until very hot then put the potatoes on in a single layer.
4. Roast and turn them now and again, for 50-60 minutes until browned on all sides with crispy edges.
5. Serve in paper cones (newspaper or baking paper) with the fish along with vinegar and salt.

Great Britain

Tea Scones

>2 cups sifted flour
>2 tbsp sugar
>3 tsp baking powder
>½ tsp salt
>1/3 cup butter
>1 egg, beaten
>¾ cup milk, approximately

1. Preheat oven to 425° F.
2. Sift together the flour, sugar, baking powder, and salt.
3. Chop in the butter with a pastry blender until the flour resembles coarse cornmeal.
4. Add the egg and about ¾ of the milk. Stir quickly and lightly, only until no flour shows. Add more milk if needed to make a soft dough.
5. Turn the dough out on a floured surface and knead gently. Cut the dough in half. Shape each half into a ball and press into a ½ inch thick round. Cut into eight wedges like a pie.
6. Place wedges on a parchment paper lined sheet with pieces not touching. Bake until deep golden brown, about 12 minutes. Makes 16 scones. *Nuts and orange zest can be added to the dough before kneading.*

Cucumber Sandwiches

>1 English cucumber
>mayonnaise
>goat cheese
>butter
>white sandwich bread cut into rounds

1. Thinly slice cucumber.
2. Cut bread with a cookie cutter into rounds.
3. Spread mayonnaise, butter or goat cheese on both sides to seal the bread and prevent bread from getting soggy.
4. Place the cucumbers (3) slices on the edge of the bread.
5. Serve with tea and scones, clotted cream and jam.

Stable *to* Table

Welsh Cob

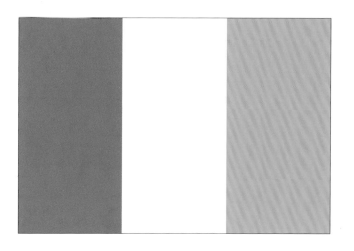

Ireland

**IRISH DRAUGHT HORSE
CONNEMARA**

Spring Garden Salad with Lemon Vinaigrette
Hay Roasted Spring Lamb
Mint Pesto Sauce
Irish Coffee
Strawberry Soup

Stable *to* Table

Spring Garden Salad

fresh herbs
baby lettuce
edible flowers

This meadow salad is made up of Mesclun (its name comes from mescal, meaning to "mix") and many fresh herb and baby lettuces such as arugula, radicchio, chicory, chervil, frisee, escarole, many which are included in ready-made mixtures. Toss in some edible flowers such as rose petals, pansies, nasturtiums, violets, squash blossoms, chive flowers. Serve with a lightly tossed lemon vinaigrette.

Lemon Vinaigrette

1 ½ tbsp white wine vinegar
1 ½ tbsp dry white wine
2 tbsp lemon juice
½ cup sunflower oil
½ cup extra virgin olive oil

Whisk the vinegar, wine and juice in a bowl until combined. Slowly whisk in oils until combined. Season to taste. *The vinaigrette will keep in the fridge for up to one week.*

Irish Draught

Stable *to* Table

Hay Roasted Spring Lamb

4 handfulls of fresh alfalfa soaked in water
stems of fresh herbs
(rosemary, mint, thyme, oregano, parsley)
I boneless leg of lamb wrapped
Kosher salt
I head of garlic
2 cups water
whole new or fingerling potatoes

The aroma of spring lamb roasted on a bed of fresh cut hay and herbs will have your taste buds hopping all over your tongue. This method of roasting has been done for 1,000 years, lending the smells of spring to the roasted meat while retaining the juices.

1. Place a roasting rack in roasting pan. Make a nest of rinsed alfalfa, along with the fresh herbs, on the roasting rack.
2. Place the seasoned and garlic pierced lamb on top, and cover with more wet hay.
3. Pour 2 cups of water under the rack.
4. Cover all with alumnium foil.
5. Roast at 350° F for I hr. 50 min.
6. Remove lamb from roaster (and hay) and cover with foil to rest for 20 min. Serve with roasted new and fingerling potatoes and mint pesto sauce.

ROASTED POTATOES

Toss potatoes with 3 tbsp of olive oil and roast in a 400° F oven for 30 minutes until tender.

Mint Pesto Sauce

I cup fresh mint leaves
¼ cup walnut oil
¼ cup finely ground walnuts
I clove of garlic

Combine all ingredients in food processor and refrigerate until needed.

Connemara

Stable *to* Table

Strawberry Soup

6 pint boxes of strawberries
3 limes
4 cups water
2 cups sugar
3 to 5 tbsp Balsamic vinegar
high quality vanilla ice cream

1. Boil sugar and water together until dissolved. Leave to cool.
2. Add strawberries and lime juice and blend it all together.
3. Strain it through a sieve.
4. Add balsamic vinegar for taste. Keep cold.
5. Serve with baby basil leaves and a small scoop of vanilla ice cream. *A thin wedge of chocolate brownie dusted with powdered sugar is a beautiful combination.*

Irish Coffee

1 cup hot coffee
1 ½ oz. Irish Whiskey
3 tsp sugar
whipped cream
chocolate covered coffee beans

1. Combine first 3 ingredients in a mug of choice.
2. Top with whipped cream and chocolate covered coffee beans.

Ireland

Morocco

ARABIAN HORSE

Hummus

Moroccan Bread

Tangine (Berber Beef Stew)

Tangier Couscous

Baladi (Mixed Salad)

Casbah Carrot Salad

Sahara Pumpkin Pie

Baklava (Pistachio Tarts)

Hummus

I can of chickpeas rinsed and drained
¼ cup tahini
I clove, peeled and crushed with ½ tsp course salt
¼ cup fresh lemon juice or more to taste
I to 2 tbsp olive oil
ground cumin, hot paprika, or pomegranate seeds

A good plate of hummus is never presented undressed. A mixture of heated oil and paprika is also a beautiful presentation drizzled around the plate.

1. Rinse and drain chickpeas. Place in food processor.
2. Stir up the tahini in its jar with the oil until well blended.
3. Blend the tahini, garlic, and lemon juice until the mixture "whitens."
4. With machine running, add ¼ cup water. Add chickpeas and lemon juice and process until well blended. Season to taste.
5. To serve as a dip, spread on a shallow serving dish. Use the back of a spoon to make a well in the center, drizzle with olive oil, and sprinkle with cumin, hot paprika, or pomegranate seeds.

Moroccan Bread

A flat bread that can be purchased in most speciality stores. Just heat and serve with the meal.

© Sparagowski

Arabian

Stable *to* Table

Tangine (Berber Beef Stew)

2 lbs. cubed beef
1 onion chopped
2 cloves of garlic minced
2 tbsp olive oil
2 carrots sliced diagonally
2 medium zucchini, sliced
2 cups diced sweet potatoes or butternut squash
1 can chickpeas rinsed and drained
1 bay leaf
1 tbsp tumeric
1 tbsp cinnamon
1 tbsp cumin
½ cup raisins
1 can (14 1/2 oz.) diced tomatoes
4 cups beef broth
cilantro for garnish

1. Brown beef in batches in enough oil to lightly cover the dutch oven. *Over crowding causes beef to boil instead of brown.*
2. Add onions and garlic and cook for 3 min.
3. Stir in tumeric, cinnamon, cumin, and 1 bay leaf.
4. Add 4 cups of beef broth and can of diced tomatoes. Simmer for 15 min.
5. Add the sliced carrots, sweet potato, zucchini, and the drained chickpeas. Simmer on low for 10 min.
6. Serve over couscous. Garnished with cilantro, mint or parsley. Serves 8.

Couscous

Couscous is the Moroccan national dish. It is granules of semolina but can be made with other grains. Boiled and steamed in 5 minutes, it is always served with the tagine. It can be purchased in the grain section in most grocery stores. One can prepare Moroccan couscous in the Berber style, with chicken, turnips, and creamy milk or as a dessert with dates, cinnamon, and sugar. Fez couscous can be spicy with chili peppers and ground pepper as well as a sweet version with onions, raisins, chickpeas and lamb. A perfect harmony!

Morocco

Arabian

Stable *to* Table

Casbah Carrot Salad

7 large carrots, scraped and grated

4 tbsp granulated sugar

4 tbsp lemon juice

orange-flower water

pinch of salt

1. Mix the carrots with the sugar, lemon juice, orange-flower water, and salt.
2. Marinate 1 hour before serving.
   Serves 8.

Arabian

Stable *to* Table

Arabian

Baladi (Mixed Salad)

4 ripe tomatoes, sliced

1 red onion, sliced thinly

1 green bell pepper, sliced thinly

1 cucumber, sliced thinly

chopped parsley

2 tbsp olive oil

2 tbsp white wine vinegar

1 tbsp of lemon juice

salt and pepper to taste

1. Line a salad bowl with boston bibb lettuce.
2. Arrange sliced tomatoes vertically around the bowl.
3. Fill the center of the bowl with cucumber, green bell pepper and red onion slices.
4. Sprinkle top with chopped parsley.
5. For the dressing, whisk olive oil, vinegar, lemon juice, salt and pepper. Serves 8.

Sahara Pumpkin Pie

2 envelopes unflavored gelatin
1 cup evaporated milk
1 cup canned or mashed cooked pumpkin
½ tsp pumpkin pie spice
¼ tsp grated orange rind
¾ cup plain yogurt
2 eggs (separated)
1/8 tsp salt
2/3 cup firmly packed brown sugar

GINGERSNAP CRUST
1 cup gingersnap crumbs
2 tbsp melted butter
vegetable cooking spray

Combine crumbs and melted butter in a small bowl; stir well. Firmly press mixture into 9" pie plate coated with cooking spray. Yield: one 9-inch crust

1. Sprinkle gelatin over milk in a heavy saucepan; let stand 1 minute.
2. Cook over low heat, stirring constantly until gelatin dissolves.
3. Add pumpkin pie spice, egg yolks and grated orange rind; stir well.
4. Chill until the consistency of unbeaten egg white.
5. Fold in yogurt (at room temperature).
6. Beat egg whites (at room temperature) and salt at medium speed of an electric mixer until soft peaks form.
7. Add brown sugar, a little at a time, and beat until stiff peaks form. Fold in egg white mixture.
8. Pour into Gingersnap Crust, and chill.
9. Sprinkle pie with pecans for garnish before serving. Serves 8.

Baklava (Pistachio Tarts)

Baklava (purchased in bakeries and grocery stores)

dates

almonds

grapes

sliced oranges

SYRUPY ESPRESSO COFFEE

Ground nutmeg, cinnamon, and cloves can be added when making the coffee. Add ¼ teaspoon to every I oz. ground coffee before making coffee in your usual fashion.

MINT TEA

To make a I ½ pt. pot (enough for 6 glasses) rinse the pot with boiling water and then throw this water away. Put I tablespoon green tea, I oz. sugar and a handful of fresh mint. Cover with boiling water and allow the tea to brew for at least 3 minutes. Pour out into a glass and correct the sweetness. Sip, talk and enjoy!

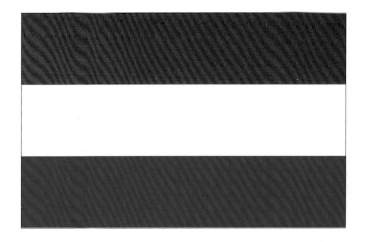

The Netherlands

DUTCH WARMBLOOD
FRIESIAN

Dutch Split Pea Soup
Dutch Noodles
Gevulde Kool (Dutch Stuffed Cabbage)

Dutch Warmblood

Stable *to* Table

Dutch Split Pea Soup

I lb. dried green split peas
I ½ quarts cold water
¼ cup diced salt pork
½ cup chopped leeks
½ cup chopped celery
½ cup chopped onions
I bay leaf
2 tsp salt
I smoked ham hock
chopped parsley

1. Rinse and sort peas. Place peas in a large pot and cover with water to soak over night or boil for 2 minutes and soak I hour.
2. In a large skillet cook salt pork for 5 minutes.
3. Add the vegetables and cook 10 minutes until soft but not brown.
4. Add salt pork mixture, bay leaf, salt and ham hock to the peas. Cover and slowly bring to a boil. Reduce heat and simmer for 2 hours until the ham hock separates from the bone.
5. Remove ham hock meat reserve and discard the bone and bay leaf. Strain the soup and puree in a blender.
6. Return the meat to the pot and adjust seasonings. Add the ham and sliced sausages and simmer 5 minutes longer. Serve hot and garnished with chopped parsley.

The Netherlands

Fresian

Dutch Noodles

½ cup blanched almonds
3 tbsp butter
3 tbsp poppy seeds
1 tbsp lemon juice
8 oz. cooked noodles
salt and pepper

1. Sliver almonds and saute until browned.
2. Melt the butter, add the almonds, poppy seeds and lemon juice and pour over noodles.
3. Add salt and cayenne and toss together. Serves 4-6.

Gevulde Kool (Dutch Stuffed Cabbage)

1 small head cabbage
¾ lb. ground pork
¼ lb. beef or veal
2 slices of bread soaked in water
1 tsp salt
ground black pepper
nutmeg to taste
2 tbsp butter

1. Remove eight to ten outer leaves from the cabbage and cook them in boiling salt water 10 min.
2. Drain cooked cabbage and put a leaf or two on a square of double folded cheesecloth.
3. Mix the meats with bread and seasonings.
4. Put a thin layer of meat on the cabbage, cover with a leaf or two, add another layer of meat until all the meat and cabbage leaves are used.
5. Gather the four corners of the cloth and tie. Lower in boiling salted water and cover for 1 ½ hrs.
6. Preheat oven to 400° F.
7. Remove cabbage from cloth and place on a greased baking dish. Dot with butter and place in oven until lightly browned.

Dutch Warmblood

Stable *to* Table

Portugal

LUSITANO

Bacalhau (Portuguese Cod, Wine, and Potato Casserole)

Portuguese Roasted Tomatoes and Garlic

Caldo Chourico (Portuguese Sausage, Kale and Bean Soup)

Arroz Doce (Portuguese Rice Pudding)

Bacalhau
(Potuguese Cod, Wine and Potato Casserole)

1 ½ lbs. fresh cod
2 yellow onions sliced
3 tbsp Olive oil
2 garlic cloves
3 potatoes boiled and sliced
4 roma tomatoes
1 tsp chili pepper
1 bay leaf
¾ cup white wine
½ cup vegetable broth
2 allspice crushed
salt and pepper
2 tbsp parsley
chopped garlic

1. In a large skillet, brown the onions in the olive oil. Add the garlic for 1 min. Remove and save onions and garlic.
2. Season the cod with salt and pepper and cut in serving pieces. Brown in same skillet with a little more oil for 1 min. on each side.
3. Add saved onions and garlic, chopped tomatoes, chili pepper, bay leaf, allspice, wine and broth. Simmer for 5 min. Season with salt and pepper.
4. In a terracotta baking dish layer the peeled, boiled and sliced potatoes with the fish mixture. Cover with top and finish in a 350° F oven for 25 min. Serves 6.
If you are using the terracotta dish be sure to soak it in water for 15 min.

Portuguese Roasted Tomatoes and Garlic

6 Roma tomatoes
olive oil
salt and pepper

1. Half the tomatoes lengthwise. Put on a lined cookie sheet. Drizzle with olive oil and salt and pepper. Roast in the oven at 400° F for 30 min.
Use for garnish on the cod casserole along with the roasted garlic.
2. Wrap a head of garlic (with a drizzle of olive oil) in aluminum foil and roast along with the tomatoes. Cut the soft head in two and squeeze on a slice of country bread.

Caldo Chourico
(Portuguese Sausage, Kale and Bean Soup)

1 lb. chorizo or hot Italian sausage

1 lb. sweet Italian sausage or other mild sausage

1 small chopped onion

28 oz. vegetable broth

1 can of white kidney beans or navy beans
(drained and rinsed)

1 bunch of fresh kale washed and chopped

½ cup beer or water

¼ tsp pepper or crushed red pepper

1. In a large saucepan, brown the sliced sausage and onion until tender. Drain any fat.

2. Add the vegetable broth, kale, beans, beer or water and pepper.

3. Cover and simmer for about 20 minutes. Serves 6.

Stable *to* Table

Arroz Doce (Portuguese Rice Pudding)

3 ½ cups water
8 cups milk
I cup rice
I cup sugar
2 sticks of cinnamon
pinch of salt

1. In a large sauce pan over medium, heat 3 ½ cups of water and 3 ½ cups of milk to scalding.
2. Pour in the rice and cook over medium heat.
3. When the rice is tender, stir in the sugar, cinnamon sticks and the rest of the scalded milk. Stir and cook until the desired consistency.
4. Remove cinnamon sticks and add a pinch of salt.
5. Serve at room temperature on a platter with a traditional cinnamon design sprinkled on top. Serves 6-8.

   A purchased stencil design has a beautiful presentation.

Lusitano

Spain

ANDALUSIAN   Gazpacho Andaluz
                 Paella Aurora
                 Flan Aurora

Stable *to* Table

Gazpacho Andaluz

4 large ripe peeled tomatoes
2 slices bread, crusts removed
½ cup chopped green bell pepper
1 peeled and seeded cucumber
½ cup onion
2 cloves garlic
4 tbsp olive oil
2 tsp salt
5 tbsp sherry vinegar
1 - 2 cups of water

1. Cut the peeled tomatoes into chunks and put them in a blender or processor along with the peppers, cucumber and onion all chopped and add the garlic. Puree all together and add the bread then slowly add the oil until incorporated.
2. Then add the salt and vinegar. Taste and correct the seasonings.
3. Stir in the cold water.
4. Chill the gazpacho until serving time. Serves 6-8.
   Garnishes: Typically, gazpacho is accompanied by small bowls of chopped tomatoes, chopped onions, chopped peppers, small croutons of toasted bread, diced and chopped eggs, and chopped cucumbers.
   A hot Spanish Andalusian summer means cold gazpacho. When we lived in the small town of Moron de la Frontera, gazpacho was the basic fare of Andalusian peasants. Tourists and upper classes soon decided the fabulous tastes should come out of the fields and onto the restaurant tables.

Andalusian

Paella Aurora

I dozen clams or mussels (or canned)

2 lbs. large shrimp with shells and heads

½ lb. peeled medium shrimp

2 chicken breasts

½ lb. pork loin cut in cubes

I lb. chorizo sliced

¼ cup olive oil

3 cloves of garlic

I bay leaf

2 cups chopped onion

½ cup chopped bell pepper

½ cup chopped celery

2 large tomatoes, peeled seeded and chopped (or I can of diced tomatoes)

3 cups rice white or packaged yellow saffron rice

6 cups hot chicken broth

½ tsp saffron (if using white rice)

black pepper

2 tsp salt

½ tsp paprika

3 large jarred red whole peppers

I cup cooked green peas

1. Clean the clams or mussels and steam them open. Discard any that did not open.

2. On a baking sheet lay the large shelled shrimp in one layer and drizzle olive oil, salt and pepper. Roast at 450° F for 5 min. or until shrimp are pink and a little crisp. Remove and save for garnish on top of the finished paella.

3. Brown the chicken, pork, and sausage in a large heavy skillet. Add the medium peeled shrimp for I min. Set all meats aside.

4. Add the onion, peppers, garlic, and bay leaf to the oil. Sautee until soft but not brown. Add the rice until the grains are somewhat opaque, stirring constantly so they don't stick. Add the tomatoes and chicken broth along with the saffron, salt, pepper, and paprika. Add the meats and stir until combined.

5. Cover and put into a 350° F oven for about 20 min. or until the liquid has been absorbed. Remove from oven and stir in the peas and a small jar of pimientos. Let sit for 10 minutes before pouring mixture into a large paella pan.

6. Decorate top with the clams or mussels, large shrimp and strips of red pimiento. Hollow out a fresh red pepper and fill it with shrimp (tails inside and heads on the outside) Alternate shrimp and pimientos around the pan. Slice lemons for squeezing on the served paella.

Presentation is as important as the taste!

Spain

Andalusian

Stable *to* Table

Flan Aurora

¾ cup sugar

4 large eggs

3 slices white bread crusts removed

1 (14 oz.) can of sweetened condensed milk

1 (8 oz.) container mascarpone cheese (1 cup)

1 cup evaporated milk

2/3 cup water

3 tbsp butter melted

1 tsp vanilla extract

1. Sprinkle sugar in a heavy skillet. Cook over medium heat, stirring constantly with a wooden spoon, until sugar melts and turns light brown. Remove from heat.

2. Quickly pour hot caramel into 9" round cake pan, tilting to coat bottom; set pan aside. Caramel will harden and crack.

3. Combine eggs and remaining 7 ingredients in a large food processor or blender. Process just until smooth.

4. Pour custard mixture over syrup in cake pan. Place cake pan in a large shallow pan. Cover cake pan with aluminum foil.

5. Add hot water to shallow pan to a depth of 1". Bake at 350° F for 50 to 55 minutes or until knife comes out clean. *Center should still be slightly liquid, flan will finish cooking as it cools.*

6. Remove cake pan from the water bath; cool completely on a wire rack. Cover and chill for several hours or overnight.

7. Loosen edges of flan a with a spatula; invert onto a rimmed serving plate, letting caramel sauce drizzle over the top. Top with a strawberry fan.

STRAWBERRY FANS

Choose firm red strawberries. Place a strawberry on its side on a chopping board and make 5-7 cuts in the fruit, taking care not to slice right through to the top of the berry. Using the flat side of the knife, gently press on the strawberry to "fan" it out. With the point of a knife, carefully cut or pull out the center hull. Replace it with a small sprig of fresh mint. Use for decorating desserts, ice cream, or serve with chicken salad.

Stable *to* Table

Measuring Liquids by Volume

TSP	TBSP	FLUID OZ.	CUPS	PINTS	QUARTS	GALLONS
3 tsp	1 tbsp	1/2 fluid oz.				
	2 tbsp	1 fluid oz.				
	4 tbsp	2 fluid oz.	1/4 cup			
	8 tbsp	4 fluid oz.	1/2 cup			
	16 tbsp	8 fluid oz.	1 cup			
		16 fluid oz.	2 cups	1 pint		
		32 fluid oz.	4 cups	2 pints	1 quart	
		128 fluid oz.	16 cups	8 pints	4 quarts	1 gallon

Metric Conversions by Volume

U.S.	METRIC
1 tsp	5 milliliters
1 tbsp	15 milliliters
1/4 cup	59 milliliters
1 cup	236 milliliters
1 pint	473 milliliters
1 quart	946 milliliters
1 gallon	3.8 liters

METRIC	U.S.
10 milliliters	2 tsp
30 milliliters	1 fluid oz.
100 milliliters	1/2 cup minus 1 tbsp
500 milliliters	2 cups plus 2 tbsp
1 liter	4 1/4 cups, or 1 quart plus 1/4 cup

Metric Conversions by Mass

U.S.	METRIC
1 oz.	28.35 grams
1 pound	454 grams (0.45 kilogram)

METRIC	U.S.
100 grams	3.5 oz.
500 grams	1.1 pounds (17.6 oz.)
1 kilogram	2.2 pounds (35.2 oz.)

Abbreviations

tsp	teaspoon
tbsp	tablespoon
lb.	pound
oz.	ounce

Temperature Conversions

FAHRENHEIT	CELSIUS
32° F	0° C
100° F	37.8° C
212° F	100° C
300° F	148.9° C
350° F	176.7° C
400° F	204.4° C
450° F	232.2° C

Stable to Table

Acknowledgments

The authors wish to thank the following people for their generous support in producing this book:

DAWN HARRIS BROWN *A special thanks to my husband, Gary, and dear friend Bonney for obeying my notes: "Don't eat this, it hasn't been photographed!" Thanks to Richard and Sarah Freeman and all my friends at Oak Hill Ranch for beautiful Danish Warmbloods and for being official tasters. Thanks to Sharon Londono for her access to her lovely Paso Finos. Thanks to Paola and Leonardo Orejarena for sharing their special Colombian family recipes. And of course my " mama savin' " hunter, Sweet Potato.*

CHRISTY SANANTONIO *A heartfelt appreciation goes to all who have cheered and championed with great enthusiasm as this book was being birthed. To my dear friend, Dawn Harris Brown — you are such an inspiration to me. Thank you for allowing me to embark on this epic journey and creative adventure with you. To Rachel Chotin Lincoln — your artistic abilities are beyond genius! I am grateful that you lent your brilliant talents for this book. To my husband, Jeff — I am forever indebted to you for your tireless support and encouragement in all of my endeavors in our life together.*

Photography Credits

Cover Image shot on location at Woodlawn Plantation, St. Francisville, Louisiana. Heather Blitz: author portrait with horse inside back flap. Dawn Harris Brown: pages 21-22, 30, 33, 48, 55-56, 58-59, 66, 72, 74-75, 77-78, 86, 90, 92-93, 95, 97-99, 103, 105, 107, 110-112, 114-115, 118-119, 121, 123. Rachel Chotin Lincoln: cover photograph, pages 2, 8-9, 10-11, 13-20, 25-26, 36-38, 42-43, 45-47, 82-85, 87, 124, author portrait with horse inside front flap, author portrait seated inside back flap. Jerry Sparagowski: Contents photograph, pages 12, 44, 49, 67, 69, 91. Eugenia Uhl: Author portrait inside front flap. Kristina Wiseman: pages 52-53, 63, 65, 68.

Horse Breeds

American Paint Horse: Cover, page 124 – Cherokee and Page 21 – Little Dude, Woodlawn Plantation, Marjorie Judd, trainer. American Quarter Horse: Inside front flap - Dawn Harris Brown with Sweet Potato. Photographed by Rachel Chotin Lincoln. Page 24 – Photographed by Todd Klassy, shutterstock.com. Page 24 – Rider Nickie Smith. Photographed by Kat Roddgers Photography. Andalusian: Pages 118-119 – Shannon Gillette on her dancing Andalusian stallion. Photographed by Dawn Harris Brown. Page 122 – Photographed by Makarova Viktoria (Vikarus), shutterstock.com. Appaloosa: Page 27 – Photographed by Lenkadan, shutterstock.com. Arabian: Page 91 – Photographed by Jerry Sparagowski. Page 95 – Mrs. Judy Sirbasku's Rhapsody in Black. Photographed by Randy Clark. Pages 94, 96-97 – Photographed by Olga_i, shutterstock.com. Camargue: Page 54 – Photographed by Lebanmax, shutterstock.com. Connemara: Page 86 – Photographed by Ivica Drusany, shutterstock.com. Cutting Horse: Lida McAllister with her horse Chicka Tari. Danish Warmblood: Inside Back Flap – Christy Sanantonio riding her gelding, Grenadier. Photographed by Heather Blitz. Page 44 – Oak Hill Ranch's Rambo. Photographed by Jerry Sparagowski. Page 46 – Hil Cat Farm's Willemoes. Photographed by Megan Burgess. Page 49 – Heather Blitz on Rambo. Photographed by Jerry Sparagowski. Dutch Warmblood: Page 102 – Zamantha HF. Photographed by Alicia Frese. Page 106 – Photographed by Zuzule, shutterstock.com. Fresian: Page 104 – Photographed by Lenkadan, shutterstock.com. Hackney Pony: Page 73 – Photographed by Perry Correll, shutterstock.com. Hanoverian: Page 62 – Photographed by Abramova Kseniya, shutterstock.com. Irish Draught: Page 83 – Mr. Irvin I. (Skip) Crawford, II, Master of the Potomac Hunt on Dandelion Diamond Rebel. Photographed by Renee Lenkin. Lipizzan: Page 31 – Photographed by Dr. Ajay Kumar Singh, shutterstock.com. Page 32 – Photographed by Ventura, shutterstock.com. Lusitano: Page 113 – Photographed by Miguel Azevedo e Castro, shutterstock.com. Page 115 – Chaos Interagro. Photographed by Tupa. Oldenberg: Pages 67, 69 – Oak Hill Ranch's Solos Landtinus. Photographed by Jerry Sparagowski. Paso Fino: Page 39 – Sharon Londono's Exodo. Photographed by Cheri Prill. Polo Pony: Page 22 – Skull Valley Polo Club, Arizona. Page 23 – Dr. C. Paul Harris, Sr., taken in 1938 in Houston, Texas. Selle Francais: Page 57 - Cavalry at a military parade celebrating Bastille Day on the Champs Elysees in Paris, France. Photographed by Migel, shutterstock.com. Shetland Pony: Page 76 – Photographed by Pirita, shutterstock.com. Thoroughbred: Page 12 – Photographed by Jerry Sparagowski. Page 17 – Race day at Keeneland. Photographed by Rachel Chotin Lincoln. Trakehner: Page 64 – Photographed by Gustavo Miguel Fernandes, shutterstock.com. Welsh Cob: Page 79 – Photographed by Groomee, shutterstock.com.

Stable *to* Table

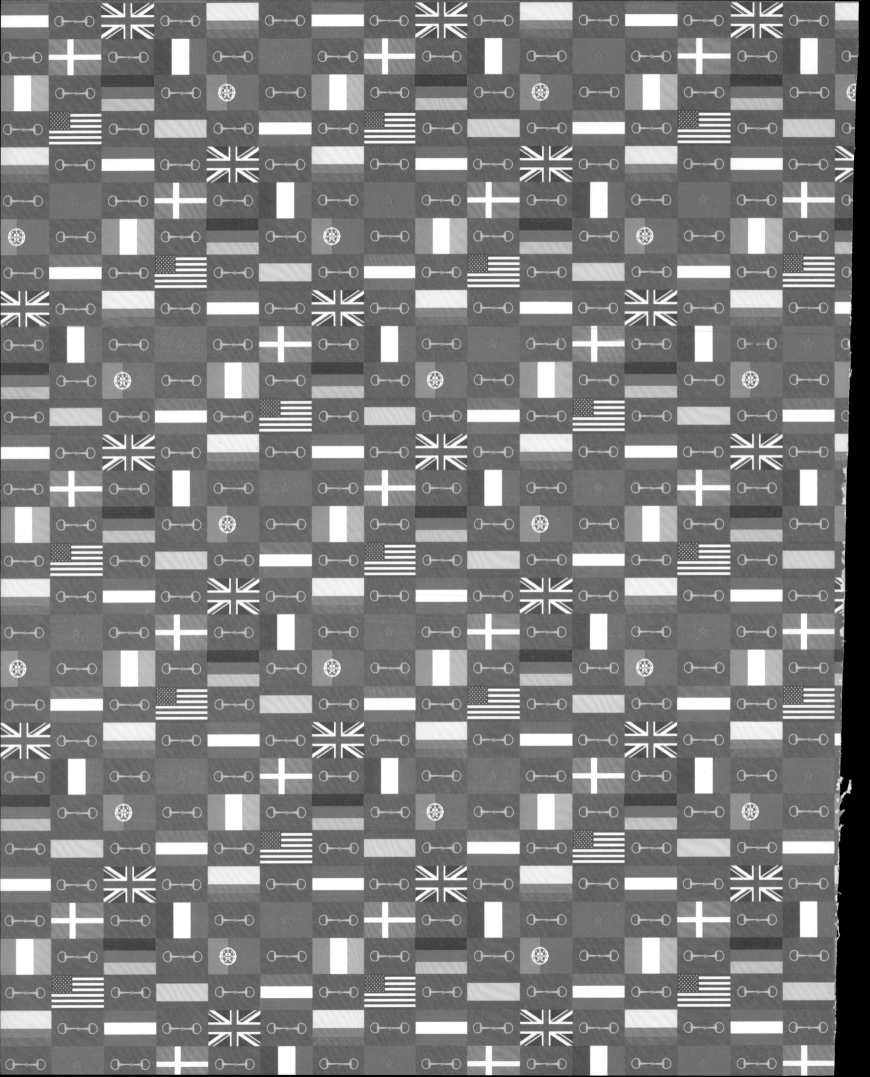